MASTERING THE SALES GAME:

A New Strategy

Melissa R. Rodriguez

All rights reserved. No part of this publication may be reproduced, distributed, or transmitted in any form or by any means, including photocopying, recording, or other electronic or mechanical methods, without the prior written permission of the publisher, except in the case of brief quotations embodied in critical reviews and certain other noncommercial uses permitted by copyright law.

Copyright © Melissa R. Rodriguez, 2023.

Table of Contents

Foreword

Chapter 1: Understanding Your Customers

Chapter 2: Crafting Your Unique Sales Pitch

Chapter 3: Building Strong Relationships

Chapter 4: Closing Deals and Achieving Success

Chapter 5: Staying Ahead of the Competition

Final Tips

Foreword

Allow me to ask you a question. The last time you put in motion your goods to sell on the net, or even offline, how did you determine what price you were going to be distributing at?

At a guess, I'd likely assume you glanced at the rivals to see what they were charging. While this is a terrific beginning, it's far from the complete picture, and you're fumbling in the dark if you look at rivalry as the only component you're taking into consideration.

Do you comprehend you may double your sales volume by doubling your price? I've done it myself, and I'll illustrate how.

Do you also comprehend that 99% of the things I see being marketed are too cheap? So much so, that they're turning purchasers off rather than enticing them (which is no doubt what they believe they're doing).

Let's drive out some pricing fallacies and go right down to the facts to guarantee you receive the most money in your pocket the next time you put in action one of your items.

There are a few items that I desire to speak to you about relating to pricing before you walk out, construct a sales system, set up a site and stuff a price on your product.

Getting Started

This Book attempts to provide a few insights into the adaptability you have as a net marketer with your items. The trouble is, most folks just appear to put a price on their things with little time wasted analyzing it, why they've priced it like this, and what variables are going to contribute to whether it's a successful option.

Sounds complex and a lot of work? Well, let me tell you it's not.

However, I believe I must demonstrate how much flexibility you have to experiment with pricing, and the consequences of getting it wrong in a variety of ways, so before you set a price on your product and release it to the public, take a few moments to read, pick up the points, and consider them using them as a checklist.

Now understand, there's a far wider picture to this than most people comprehend. A lot of the time prices are set there, simply as they may be, and potentially fitted loosely around competitors and additional items and services supplying comparable issues, nevertheless, it's not simply about planting a number and a dollar sign behind it. All through this method you need to be asking yourself heaps of why queries. A few times, someone asks me why the heck I go so in-depth into things and speak about why they occur. They just desire to learn how to create a big load of money quickly.

Well, I say to them I may teach you how to do something, but if the condition of circumstances changes, and you didn't understand why it worked in the first place, then you're going to have to come straight back to me once again to figure out how to do the same thing in another method. But, if I teach you how issues function, you may take this information and comprehend that you can adapt to the fast-paced shifting world of the company online or offline. If you can't accommodate, you're dead.

As I say, there's quite a lot to this, and a lot of topics that we're going to address, and there's going to be a load of questions that are going to jump into your brain. Does rivalry matter in such a huge marketplace about pricing? Ought I be cheaper? Ought I be more expensive? How do I grasp when to be which and why? Should I make specific deals with certain categories of individuals? Who? Why? Ought to provide diverse versions of my goods at distinct prices? How can I achieve it, and how do I comprehend whether I'm doing it right?

There are a bunch of answers concerning the above and much more that I'm going to provide you in a minute. But via this, I want you to keep in mind the freedom you have as a net marketer with your price. Get this properly, and it may easily mean twice the earnings for you. Get it wrong, and you'll likely have difficulties selling anything at all.

Rules And Choices

Too many folks are scared to take the plunge and pay for their things as they feel they're worth it. Too many people notice competition and assume they have to cost less else no one is going to purchase their goods, or they'll earn less cash off of it.

This is plain, not true. Don't devalue yourself only to be cheaper. If you have a superior product, you slap a greater price tag on it. The testing and playing around to discover the ideal mix of offers, bargains, follow-up, and price decisions may come later.

Understand This

I may show you so many things that are out there properly now, in competition with one another, nonetheless, one is charging a heck of a lot more than the other.

How about the newest acquisition you made for your house, whether it was a full worktop, a new garage door, a toaster, or a dining table, whatever it was? I suppose if you consider it, you'll find that things have changed.

A long time ago, even before I was born, folks sought things that functioned. They were merely ok. However, nowadays that's not enough. It's got to be the greatest, the quickest, the prettiest, and the easiest to employ. There's a legitimate demand for luxury items developing. Make certain you don't put yours in the discount bin if it's designed as a quality product, not a bargain basement good.

Now I desire to cover something else that's infrequently done, especially in the realm of network marketing and info items, and that's supplying several priced options from the start.

Sure folks may adjust their pricing, put it up and down to experiment, put on deals, and so forth; but that's not accomplishing much if your initial idea isn't properly thought out.

Even with the simplest of single-sale knowledge goods like this, you're given alternatives. The more, the better to be honest. Whether you're a high price item supplying smaller portions to be paid at long times, or a low-cost membership site that does the reverse and gives a big fee that delivers access for 3 months, 6 months, or even a year.

Remember, the sales method is all about addressing the customer's inquiries, and squashing their anxieties or any reasons they may come up with in their heads for not acquiring your goods. It's no good you sell someone on something and then they learn they don't have the payment option they desire.

Make careful you include multiples of these. It's simple, if there's anyone out there with a site that just provides one payment method, they're losing business. Don't let this be you.

Never, regardless of what you do, neglect the folks who have purchased from you previously. It's not hard to come up with methods to reward them. Correctly now, I'm putting together an ID number structure for myself that permits prior consumers to come around and buy my products at a reduced cost.

These folks are the most vital of all. You've already got them on your lists, and they've previously bought your goods, which implies they're willing to spend cash, and naturally they trust you, and they're serious about wanting more knowledge, or the items and services you give. Remember this, since if you forget you'll go bankrupt. It's as simple as that.

You need to keep the consumers who are buying from you pleased, and you need to remain in contact with them. If you don't go out of your way to please them, you'll have to go out and spend more on locating new customers. Look after them, since they'll be with you for a long time and will form the cornerstone of a successful firm from the word go.

Adding Value

Forever increasing value. Remember while coming up with a cost for your product; don't allow it to be the sole product. The strange statement really, but examine it this way, what type of items are going to enable you to step up your pricing and urge others to acquire your product at the same time?

Get A Handle On It

The excellence of your goods and sales method is evident, but, how about bonuses? What about testimonials from established and trusted persons in your field?

It's not only material goods either. What about your reputation and how other people regard you? So here's a little advice for you. If you believe that your product isn't worth the $400 you're asking then improve its value with these strategies. If you still don't believe it's worth it, then at this point, you know that you're charging a little much for it.

Ok, I'll be frank with you. If you intend to achieve and get your pricing to perfection, without being 'cheap' you have to put in a little effort. Some research and a little mental effort. It's not everything above board one two three. Understand that it's not about being cheaper than everyone else; it's about pricing your product appropriately based on competition, who you're targeting your product at, its caliber, and your research and monitoring findings.

By now you need to have a clear concept of how much you desire to charge, and how you're going to go about it. If you have, excellent. Simply remember, the price you put out there on launch day doesn't have to be fixed in stone by trick or by crook. It's there to be fooled about and played with by you until you feel it's correct, and your testing shows you that it's right. Have a little confidence in your items. Next time you generate that fantastic info product, membership site, or piece of software, try to avoid selling it at discounted costs, as I guarantee you, it's not earning you sales, it's losing them.

There are several approaches to confer value to your goods, and the means and tactics are continually evolving via fresh and unique twists on present ideas.

It's worth looking out for them the next time you get a great sales message from a trustworthy marketer, and ask yourself, how are they adding value to their products?

Watching how other people do things on their sites is one of the most beneficial cost-free and pretty much effort-free techniques of research that you have in your arsenal, nevertheless, it works exceptionally well. Keep it in mind all the time.

Techniques To Keep Value High For Better Pricing

To acquire the proper pricing for your items you have to have the correct value. Here are the strategies to make your product more valuable to your consumers.

The Strategies

A smart place to start here is cut-off dates and restricted quantities for your sales mailings. Likely the most utilized and publicly recognized apart from testimonials, this one gets the sales flowing if done properly.

All the cut-off dates ask for is a message that a certain deal is expiring on a given day, giving the idea that the reader will lose out if they don't acquire now, an age-old and well-used, show ever successful, method of hammering home more purchases.

If you employ this strategy, use wording that shows that your cheap price and specific offer are only guaranteed until a certain date, so that if you decide to continue at a later date, it doesn't generate a commotion, and you can avoid using those small java codes that advance the date ahead every day based on the computer clock time at the visitors end.

And second, consider limiting numbers, only letting a certain amount of people access your site at a specific moment in time. Again, fairly commonly employed, and both cater to impulsive buying and increasing value. One of my former sites had this method set up, and yet to this day, I get people asking if there's a place available yet, and even paying more cash than the regular charge to get in.

Now you may think that I'm losing cash on such a transaction, only allowing folks in a tiny number at a time, but, it doesn't occur that way. The reason the restriction was established in the first place was so that I'd have time to begin working on other projects and could run my other sites on automatic pilot, so you could say I found this one by mistake. Don't forget that you can always increase and decrease your limitations if you do this, which I strongly encourage you to attempt, even if restricting numbers doesn't fit your state of things, limiting numbers at a lesser price, very likely will suit each situation.

The next means of imparting merit is testimony. A normal amount of text is either ideally positioned on your sales letter, along the side of your nav bar, or perhaps a complete area devoted to buyer remarks and testimonials. This performs wonders for evidence of your product's capabilities and adds value.

Next up, normal incentives. Again, let's not dwell on the essentials of this because we've previously examined them, but how about pushing typical bonus gifts a little further?

How about producing a little training series that lets the customer give it away developing your reputation, as well as adding value to the original sale? Or, how about putting anything together that will generate cash by teaching the purchaser? For instance, giving a means of an affiliate marketing lesson to your consumers to assist them to become better affiliates, and ideally, push your item and earn you cash at the same time.

Always attempt to put something together that will benefit you as well as the customer, whether it's more sales, a re-branded product filled with affiliate links or connections to your product they may give away, or an instructional item that will assist your buyer, and put cash in your pocket at the same time.

While we're talking about providing incentives to boost your product. I've seen several successful products that are made up of a collection of incentives, with no actual focal point of emphasis. Naturally, they have a common topic and are all connected in some form, but, this is something to have in mind. As long as all the items complement one other, and are relevant, they may come together to produce a completely fresh product and revenue stream for yourself.

Don't increase value to the point of taking it away. Imagine if I tried to offer you a bonus with this and told you it was called 'Business Now" and then went ahead and told you it's worth five hundred.

If you've considered it, tried to find anything to throw in as a wonderful valuable addition to try to nudge consumers over the line and you honestly can't find anything outstanding about it that meets the description, go with nothing. No incentives are better than one that turns all your consumers off. As clear as it looks, it seems to be happening progressively frequently.

Following is your pricing. Have you ever seen those items that tell you that their product is worth 500 dollars, and then crossed out next to it is a fresh price with the original check out of $250, then that price wiped out, and next to it is a $20 price tag? I believe people are smarter than a lot of sales letters give them credit for.

There's nothing wrong with utilizing this, but $500 to $20? Not! The reply is either 'yeah right, this is a hoax', or more commonly, what's the catch, or 'Ok what's wrong with it?' Simply you're discounting to the point of generating uncertainty in the purchaser's head again.

See how adding a little much value too soon, or going totally over the top may be detrimental? Where you view it as offering the consumer a discount, they're perceiving it as a different question in their heads. A new obstacle that consumers need to pass, or a question they have to seek the solution to before they buy your goods. It's everywhere today. Discounts aren't awful on their own, but in this type of case, they're going to destroy your sales. Most individuals don't even know why. If you didn't before, now you do. Do not make the same mistake.

It's vital to remember to enhance value by employing incentives in a method that makes your incentives look like actual items themselves, but never lose sight of what you desire your site to achieve. Don't send folks off in various ways and have them read 10 sales letters for different items.

A further approach to enhancing worth: providing discounts for extra purchases at the checkout. Add this to your basket, then buy them together and save 50%, a great and simple technique of earning double sales in a lot of scenarios.

If this is the first thing you're manufacturing, it doesn't harm to reciprocate loyalty. How about offering them 10% off the next thing they buy from your business?

Something that's relatively underestimated and seldom ever employed is rewarding loyalty.

Most notably, if you take nothing else away from today, I want you to remember one thing, and that's that nothing in business is set in stone. No laws that exist today will exist indefinitely, nothing that works now will work eternally. Experiment, invent, and be distinctive and you'll be recognized, and earn handfuls of money.

Introduction to the Sales Game

The Sales Game refers to the process of selling items or services to consumers, trying to gain maximum profits. The sales game comprises many actions such as lead creation, customer contact management, product knowledge, completing deals, and negotiating rates. Effective salespeople must exhibit good communication, interpersonal, and problem-solving abilities, as well as the ability to recognize consumer requirements and modify their sales presentations appropriately. Success in the sales game involves a mix of plan, effort, and tenacity.

In addition to the aforementioned abilities, effective salespeople generally maintain a growth attitude and consistently endeavor to enhance their skills and knowledge. This may require attending training sessions, reading industry journals, and remaining up-to-date on market developments and competition. It is also crucial for salespeople to have a deep awareness of their products and services, as well as the distinctive selling features that separate them from rivals.

The sales process often starts with finding prospective customers and cultivating connections via numerous touch points such as phone calls, emails, and face-to-face meetings. The final aim is to clinch a contract and secure the sale. This involves good communication and persuasive abilities, as well as the ability to overcome objections and negotiate advantageous conditions.

The sales game is a competitive sector and success is generally assessed by criteria such as the number of transactions completed, sales volume, and customer happiness. Sales teams may also create objectives and performance incentives to increase enthusiasm and encourage continual development.

The Challenges of Modern Sales

The current sales environment provides various obstacles, including:

- ***Increased competitiveness***

Increased competitiveness in the current sales environment offers a big challenge for sales teams. With the plethora of information accessible online, buyers may study and compare goods and services before reaching out to salespeople. This implies that sales teams must separate themselves from their competition to earn the sale.

Additionally, the growth of e-commerce and online marketplaces has made it simpler for new companies to join the market and compete with existing businesses. Sales teams must, therefore, be prepared to fight not just with conventional rivals but also with new, nimbler players.

- ***Evolving purchasing behavior***

The behavior of buyers is continually altering, providing a big challenge for sales teams. Today's buyers are more knowledgeable, have greater expectations, and are less likely to be convinced by old sales approaches. They are wanting a more customized, consultative sales strategy that gives value and helps them solve their challenges.

Additionally, the emergence of social media and online forums has provided purchasers a platform to investigate and debate goods and services, further affecting their buying choices.

Sales teams must grasp the effect of these groups and the role they play in the purchase process.

- ***Technological advances***

Technological improvements have had a tremendous influence on the sales environment, creating both possibilities and problems for sales teams. On the one hand, new technologies have made it simpler for sales teams to obtain and analyze data, automate mundane processes, and increase the productivity of their sales process. On the other hand, the quick speed of technology development means that sales teams must consistently upskill and adapt to remain ahead of the curve.

Some of the important technology developments impacting sales include:

☆Customer relationship management (CRM) systems: These systems enable sales teams to manage customer interactions, monitor sales data, and assess performance.

☆Marketing automation: This technology helps sales teams to automate routine marketing processes, freeing up time to concentrate on high-value initiatives.

☆Artificial intelligence (AI) and machine learning: These technologies are being utilized to enhance sales forecasting, customize sales encounters and automate repetitive operations.

☆Virtual and augmented reality (VR/AR): These technologies are being utilized to improve the consumer experience and create new methods to exhibit goods and services.

- ***Data overload***

Data overload is a significant concern in the contemporary sales environment, as sales teams are presented with a rising volume of information to process and evaluate. With the development of data-driven decision-making, sales teams are expected to utilize data to guide their sales strategy but are frequently overwhelmed by the sheer amount of information available.

The difficulty of data overload is worsened by the fact that not all data is equally useful, and sales teams must be able to extract the most relevant and actionable insights from the sea of information. Additionally, many sales teams lack the knowledge and resources required to successfully evaluate data and develop significant conclusions.

- ***Remote work***

The transition towards remote work has posed new obstacles for sales teams, who are now responsible for creating and sustaining connections with customers and colleagues from a distance. Some of the primary issues of remote work for sales teams include:

☆Keeping personal connections: Building and maintaining personal ties with customers and coworkers is more challenging while working remotely.

☆Cooperation and communication: Effective collaboration and communication are vital for sales success, but may be more difficult when team members are not physically present.

☆Access to resources: Remote sales teams may have restricted access to the resources and assistance they need to be successful, such as access to databases, tools, and equipment.

☆Motivation and productivity: Maintaining motivation and productivity may be more challenging for remote sales teams, who may confront distractions and lack the structure of a regular office setting.

The Benefits of a New Strategy

Implementing a new sales strategy may provide various advantages to a corporation, including:

- *Increased efficiency*

Increased efficiency is a fundamental advantage of deploying a new sales approach. By simplifying procedures and reducing inefficiencies, a corporation may increase the productivity and effectiveness of its sales force. Here are some of the ways a new sales strategy might contribute to higher efficiency:

☆Automation: By automating monotonous processes like data input and lead generation, sales teams can concentrate on high-value activities, such as relationship development and completing transactions.

☆Better use of technology: A new sales strategy can help a firm make better use of technology, such as customer relationship management (CRM) systems, to simplify procedures and boost efficiency.

☆Improved communication: A new sales strategy can enhance communication inside the sales team and between sales and other departments, minimizing the risk of misunderstandings and delays.

☆Better targeting: A new approach can help a firm target the appropriate clients with the right message, minimizing the need for mass marketing and boosting the chance of success.

☆More effective use of time: A new approach can help sales teams prioritize their time and efforts, concentrating on the most critical tasks and optimizing their impact.

By boosting efficiency, a new sales strategy helps a corporation optimize its return on investment, cut expenses, and enhance overall performance.

- ***Improved outcomes***

Improved outcomes are another significant advantage of having a new sales approach. By generating improved sales performance, a corporation may fulfill its objectives and flourish. Here are some of the ways a fresh sales approach might lead to increased results:

☆Increased sales volume: By concentrating on the proper clients and adapting the sales approach to their demands, a new strategy enhance the number of transactions completed and total sales volume.

☆Improved market share: By keeping ahead of the curve and adjusting to changing market circumstances, a new sales strategy help a firm acquire market share and beat rivals.

☆Higher customer happiness: By identifying and addressing client demands, a new sales strategy boost customer satisfaction and raise the possibility of repeat business and referrals.

☆Better sales team performance: By giving clear guidance, incentive, and support, a new sales strategy increase the performance of the sales team and produce better outcomes.

☆Improved profitability: By improving efficiency, boosting sales volume, and decreasing expenses, a new sales strategy enhance profitability and give greater returns on investment.

A well-designed sales strategy lead to improved outcomes, including greater sales volume, enhanced market share, higher customer happiness, better sales team effectiveness, and improved profitability. By obtaining superior outcomes, a firm grow, flourish, and survive in today's competitive environment.

- ***Enhanced competitiveness***

Enhanced competitiveness is a significant advantage of adopting a new sales strategy. By keeping ahead of the curve and adjusting to changing market circumstances, a firm retain its position and grow in today's competitive industry. Here are some of the ways a new sales strategy can boost competitiveness:

☆Better grasp of the market: By continuously evaluating market trends and conditions, a new sales strategy help a firm remain informed and react to changing situations.

☆Improved product positioning: By better understanding consumer wants and customizing the sales approach appropriately, a new strategy enhances the placement of the business's goods and services in the market.

☆Increased agility: A new sales strategy make a firm more flexible and sensitive to changing market circumstances, enabling it to adjust rapidly and capitalize on new possibilities.

☆Better use of resources: A new sales strategy help a firm make better use of its resources, including time, money, and employees, to remain ahead of the competition.

☆Improved brand image: By offering clear direction and emphasis, a new sales strategy enhance the image and reputation of the firm, boosting its competitiveness and attraction to consumers.

By preserving its competitiveness, a firm may prosper and flourish in today's continuously changing business world.

- ***Better alignment with customer demands***

Better alignment with client demands is a fundamental advantage of adopting a new sales strategy. By recognizing and satisfying the demands of consumers, a firm enhance customer happiness, grow sales, and achieve long-term success. Here are some of the ways a new sales strategy can lead to improved alignment with client needs:

☆Consumer research: A new sales strategy might incorporate research and analysis to better understand customer wants and preferences, enabling the organization to modify its approach appropriately.

☆Customer segmentation: A new approach help a firm segment its clients and target them with more personalized and successful sales communications.

☆Personalization: By customizing its sales strategy and message to fit the demands of individual clients, a firm enhance the customer experience and boost sales.

☆Increased communication: A new sales strategy might involve communication and cooperation between the sales staff and other departments to better understand and react to consumer demands.

☆Customer input: By routinely seeking and evaluating client feedback, a new sales strategy help a firm remain aware and responsive to customer demands.

Better alignment with client demands is a significant advantage of adopting a new sales strategy. By recognizing and addressing consumer wants, a firm enhance customer happiness, boost sales, and achieve long-term success.

- ***Better use of resources***

Better use of resources is a major advantage of adopting a new sales strategy. By optimizing the utilization of its resources, a firm may enhance efficiency, cut expenses, and produce greater outcomes. Here are some of the ways a new sales strategy lead to greater usage of resources:

☆Targeted efforts: By concentrating on the correct consumers and sales prospects, a new sales strategy help a corporation make more successful use of its time, money, and staff.

☆Streamlined processes: A new sales strategy might involve process enhancements to remove waste and inefficiencies, enabling the organization to better use its resources.

☆Improved technology: A new strategy help a firm make greater use of technology to automate and simplify sales operations, improving productivity and decreasing expenses.

☆Increased cooperation: By promoting collaboration and communication between the sales team and other departments, a new sales strategy help the firm make better use of its resources and produce greater outcomes.

☆Effective allocation of resources: A new sales strategy might include an effective allocation of resources to guarantee that the firm is making the most of its resources to boost sales and growth.

- ***Improved team morale***

Improved team morale is a significant benefit of implementing a new sales strategy. When the sales team is motivated and engaged, it is more likely to achieve better results and drive growth for the business. Here are some of the ways a new sales strategy can lead to improved team morale:

☆Clear direction and goals: By providing clear direction and goals, a new sales strategy can help the sales team understand their role and focus their efforts.

☆Increased autonomy: A new strategy can give the sales team more control over their work and decision-making, boosting morale and motivation.

☆Improved training and support: A new sales strategy can include improved training and support to help the sales team develop new skills and succeed in their role.

☆Recognition and rewards: By recognizing and rewarding top performers, a new sales strategy can boost morale and motivate the sales team to achieve better results.

☆Collaboration and teamwork: A new strategy can foster collaboration and teamwork among the sales team, improving morale and encouraging a positive work environment.

Improved team morale is a critical benefit of implementing a new sales strategy. By boosting the motivation and engagement of the sales team, a business can achieve better results and drive growth.

- *New opportunities for growth*

New growth opportunities are a key benefit of implementing a new sales strategy. By exploring new markets, customers, and products, a business can expand its reach and drive growth. Here are some of the ways a new sales strategy can lead to new opportunities for growth:

☆Market expansion: A new sales strategy can include plans to expand into new geographic markets or target new customer segments, providing new growth opportunities.

☆Product innovation: A new strategy can encourage product innovation, leading to new and improved offerings and driving growth.

☆Strategic partnerships: A new sales strategy can include plans to form strategic partnerships with other businesses, providing access to new customers and markets.

☆Customer acquisition: By attracting and retaining new customers, a new sales strategy can drive growth and increase revenue.

☆Improved customer retention: A new strategy can include plans to improve customer satisfaction and retain existing customers, driving growth and reducing customer churn.

New growth opportunities are a critical benefit of implementing a new sales strategy. By exploring new markets, customers, and products, a business can expand its reach and drive growth.

Chapter 1: Understanding Your Customers

Understanding your customers is a vital component of a successful sales approach. By getting insights into client demands, preferences, and behavior, a firm can adjust its strategy and achieve better outcomes. Here are some of the strategies for a better knowledge of customers:

- ***Customer Research***

Customer research is the process of acquiring information about customers using different approaches, including surveys, focus groups, interviews, and data analysis. The purpose of customer research is to understand consumer requirements, preferences, habits, and attitudes, so that a company may make educated choices and enhance its goods, services, and overall customer experience.

There are various techniques for performing customer research, including:

☆Surveys: Surveys may be done using online platforms, email, or direct mail to acquire information about consumer requirements, preferences, and behavior.

☆Focus groups: Focus groups bring together a small, varied group of customers to discuss a certain product, service, or problem and obtain insights and comments.

☆Interviews: One-on-one interviews with consumers can give in-depth insights into client requirements, preferences, and behavior.

☆Data analysis: By analyzing customer data, such as purchase history and website usage, a firm can get insights into consumer preferences and behavior.

Customer research can give useful information that can inspire the creation of a new sales strategy, enhance the entire customer experience, and drive growth for the firm. By performing customer research consistently, a firm can keep up-to-date on client wants and preferences, and make educated choices that generate success.

Here are some important advantages of performing consumer research:

☆Improved consumer knowledge: By doing research, a firm can obtain useful information on customer demands, preferences, and behavior, which can assist in increasing the understanding of customers.

☆Tailored approach: With a deeper knowledge of consumers, a firm can customize its approach and message to fit the demands of individual customers, leading to enhanced customer satisfaction and loyalty.

☆Increased sales: By adapting the sales technique to fit consumer demands, a firm can improve sales and drive growth.

☆Improved customer happiness: Customer research can assist uncover areas where the firm can enhance its goods or services, resulting in higher customer satisfaction.

☆Competitive edge: By performing customer research, a firm can get a competitive advantage by knowing consumer demands better than its rivals.

- ***Customer feedback***

Client feedback is a critical element of knowing customer requirements, preferences, and happiness. By actively soliciting and using consumer feedback, organizations may make changes to their goods and services, boost customer happiness and loyalty, and drive development.

There are various techniques for getting client feedback, including:

☆Surveys: Surveys can be used to get input from a large number of consumers, and can be performed online or via the mail.

☆Focus groups: Focus groups bring together a small, varied group of consumers to discuss a certain product, service, or problem and obtain feedback.

☆Customer support interactions: Customer support contacts, such as phone calls or live chats, give a chance for consumers to express feedback in real-time.

☆Social media: Social media can be utilized to get consumer feedback by monitoring comments, reviews, and ratings on sites like Facebook, Twitter, and Yelp.

Regardless of the approach utilized, it's crucial to constantly solicit consumer feedback and act on it. This tells clients that the firm appreciates their thoughts and is devoted to offering a great experience.

Acting on client feedback might entail making adjustments to goods and services, enhancing customer assistance, or rewriting marketing materials. The objective is to leverage consumer input to consistently enhance the entire customer experience and promote company development.

By routinely collecting client input, a company can enhance its goods, services, and overall customer experience. Here are some important advantages of utilizing consumer feedback:

☆Improved customer happiness: By constantly requesting consumer input, a firm can find areas for improvement, resulting in higher customer satisfaction.

☆Increased customer loyalty: When a firm listens to customer input and makes changes based on it, consumers are more likely to feel appreciated and become more loyal.

☆Improved goods and services: Customer feedback can give significant insights into what customers want and need, helping a firm enhance its products and services.

☆Better decision-making: By incorporating customer input when making choices, a firm can guarantee that its goods and services are aligned with consumer demands and preferences.

☆Enhanced reputation: By constantly soliciting and responding to customer input, a firm may improve its image as a customer-focused corporation.

- ***Analytics***

Analytics is the practice of evaluating data and information to generate insights into corporate operations, performance, and consumer behavior. In sales, analytics is a significant tool for measuring important indicators and understanding consumer behavior, helping firms to make educated choices and achieve sales success.

Here are some ways in which analytics can be employed in sales:

☆Sales performance tracking: Analytics can be used to measure and evaluate sales performance, including the number of sales, conversion rates, and average order value. This information can be utilized to discover patterns and enhance sales operations.

☆Consumer behavior analysis: Analytics can give insight into customer behavior, including purchasing trends, product preferences, and buying behaviors. This information can be utilized to inform marketing and sales tactics.

☆Market trends analysis: Analytics can be used to monitor and evaluate market trends, including changes in consumer demand, competition activity, and market circumstances.

☆Forecasting: Analytics can be used to anticipate future sales and consumer behavior, helping firms to plan and prepare appropriately.

☆Optimization: Analytics can be utilized to discover areas for improvement and optimize sales processes, leading to higher efficiency and productivity.

To successfully apply analytics in sales, firms should leverage data-driven insights to guide their decision-making processes and regularly monitor and analyze important indicators to find trends and chances for improvement.

There are several tools and technologies available for sales analytics, including customer relationship management (CRM) systems, business intelligence software, and data visualization tools. The challenge is to use the correct tools and effectively employ analytics to acquire insights and drive sales success.

The advantages of employing analytics in sales include:

☆Improved decision-making: Analytics gives data-driven insights into sales performance and consumer behavior, helping organizations to make educated choices.

☆Higher efficiency: By evaluating data, organizations may find areas for improvement and optimize their sales processes, leading to increased efficiency and production.

☆Better consumer understanding: Analytics gives insight into customer behavior, helping firms to understand their customers better and customize their services appropriately.

☆Improved forecasting: Analytics can be used to estimate future sales and consumer behavior, enabling organizations to plan and prepare properly.

☆Increased competitiveness: By employing analytics, organizations can get a competitive advantage by leveraging data to guide their sales strategy and make educated choices.

- ***Personalization***

Personalization in sales refers to the technique of adapting the sales strategy and message to fit the particular demands and preferences of each consumer. By doing so, organizations may create stronger client connections, boost customer happiness, and drive sales success.

Here are some ways in which personalization can be done in sales:

☆Customer data and analytics: By employing customer data and analytics, organizations can obtain insights into individual customer preferences and behavior, allowing them to offer a more customized experience.

☆Customer segmentation: Customer segmentation includes breaking consumers into specific groups based on common traits, such as demographics, behavior, or preferences. By doing so, organizations can customize their sales technique and message for each group.

☆Personalized messaging: Personalized messaging entails leveraging the customer's name, location, or other information to provide a more personalized and relevant experience. This can involve email marketing, direct mail, or other types of contact.

☆Personalized offers: Personalized offers entail leveraging consumer data to generate offers that are personalized to particular client requirements and interests. This can include discounts, promotions, or other incentives.

Personalization can have a big influence on sales performance by helping firms stand out in a competitive industry, attracting and keeping consumers, and enhancing the entire customer experience. The challenge is to properly leverage personalization in a manner that matches the specific demands of each client and generates sales success.

The advantages of personalization in sales include:

☆Deeper customer connections: Personalizing the sales approach helps develop deeper, more meaningful ties with customers by displaying a genuine interest in their wants and preferences.

☆Greater consumer happiness: Personalization boost customer satisfaction by offering a more relevant and pleasurable experience, which can lead to increased customer loyalty.

☆Improved consumer engagement: Personalizing the sales approach can boost customer engagement by making the sales experience more relevant and entertaining.

☆Increased conversions: Personalization can enhance conversion rates by making the sales experience more relevant and enticing to specific consumers.

☆Competitive advantage: Personalization can give a competitive edge by helping firms stand out in a crowded marketplace and attract and keep consumers.

- ***Customer segmentation***

Customer segmentation includes examining customer data to uncover common features and behavior patterns among distinct groups of customers. This information is then utilized to generate tailored sales and marketing strategies for each category.

Here are some examples of consumer traits that may be utilized for segmentation:

☆Demographic: This contains information such as age, gender, income, education level, and profession.

☆Psychographic: This comprises information about consumers' values, beliefs, attitudes, and personality attributes.

☆Geographic: This covers information about clients' location, climate, and regional variances.

☆Behavioral: This comprises information about consumers' purchasing behaviors, preferences, and decision-making processes.

Once the client segments have been determined, firms utilize the information to design specialized sales and marketing strategies for each group. For example, a firm can build a specialized marketing campaign for a younger age, while utilizing a different technique for an older demographic.

Customer segmentation may also be used to enhance the entire customer experience by generating a more tailored and relevant experience for each group. For example, a firm may provide various discounts or incentives depending on the requirements and interests of each consumer group.

Customer segmentation is a crucial strategy for firms wanting to better their sales and marketing operations. By better understanding client demands and behavior, firms may build more effective tactics and promote sales success.

By segmenting clients, firms can:

☆Better understand customer needs: Customer segmentation helps firms obtain a better understanding of their consumers by recognizing common qualities and behaviors across distinct groups. This knowledge may then be utilized to design more successful sales tactics.

☆Tune marketing and sales efforts: By segmenting consumers into targeted groups, firms can tailor their marketing and sales efforts to fit the individual demands of each group. This may lead to greater revenue and client satisfaction.

☆Increase efficiency: Client segmentation can help organizations prioritize their efforts and allocate resources more effectively by concentrating on the most lucrative customer categories.

☆Improve customer experience: By knowing the individual requirements and preferences of each consumer group, companies can offer a more customized and relevant customer experience, leading to higher customer satisfaction and loyalty.

The Buyer's Journey

The buyer's journey is the process that a consumer goes through while making a purchase. It normally consists of three stages: awareness, consideration, and choice.

- *Awareness*

The Awareness stage of the buyer's journey is the initial step when the consumer becomes aware of a need or issue they wish to address. This is often the stage when clients start their research process, seeking information and solutions that could be able to aid them.

During this stage, clients are often seeking generic information and are not yet focused on a certain product or brand. Their major purpose is to comprehend their issue and learn more about the potential solutions accessible.

Businesses may utilize this stage to educate clients and develop brand recognition. By developing instructional material and delivering important information, companies can represent themselves as experts in their sector and create trust with prospective clients.

Examples of material that may be utilized during the Awareness stage include:

☆Blog postings that give broad information regarding a topic or issue

☆Videos that illustrate how a product or service works

☆Infographics that offer an overview of various solutions

☆Quizzes that assist clients to understand their challenges and possible solutions

It's also vital for organizations to employ the correct marketing channels to contact clients during the Awareness stage. For example, they could utilize social media, search engine optimization (SEO), or content marketing to attract a bigger audience and generate traffic to their website.

By properly connecting with clients throughout the Awareness stage, companies can establish the groundwork for a solid connection with prospective customers, and eventually, achieve more sales success.

- *Consideration*

During the Consideration stage of the buyer's journey, buyers are actively analyzing numerous possibilities and making judgments about which solutions will best fulfill their requirements. This is a vital stage in the sales process since buyers are making selections that will eventually decide whether they will pick a certain product or service.

During this stage, clients often perform considerable research and obtain information from several sources. They could compare goods and services, read reviews, seek suggestions from others, and even call out to sales personnel for further information.

Businesses can assist clients during the Consideration stage by giving educational material, such as webinars, white papers, or case studies, relevant information, and comparisons, that help buyers grasp the advantages and characteristics of competing solutions. By offering extensive product information, price comparisons, and highlighting the advantages of their solution, companies can assist clients to make educated choices and boost their chances of completing a sale.

It's also vital for firms to employ the correct marketing channels to contact clients during the Consideration stage. For example, they can utilize search engine marketing (SEM), email marketing, or display advertising to generate traffic to their website and give buyers further information.

Another crucial feature of the Consideration stage is personalization. By tailoring the sales strategy and message to fit the demands of individual consumers, organizations can help develop stronger customer connections and boost customer satisfaction. Personalization might include personalized content, product suggestions, or even customized pricing depending on the customer's unique demands and budget as discussed above.

In addition, firms should be prepared to react to client queries and give help throughout the Consideration stage. This might involve giving live chat, email support, or phone assistance to aid clients with their queries and issues.

By properly connecting with clients throughout the Consideration stage, companies can help them make educated choices and boost the odds of making a sale. By offering important information, assistance, and direction, companies may create strong connections with their consumers and position themselves as trusted advisers.

- ***Decision***

The Decision stage is the last phase in the buyer's journey and is when the consumer makes a purchase. At this stage, the consumer has done their research and is ready to make a purchase.

Businesses need to provide a seamless and good customer experience throughout the Decision stage, since this may have a big influence on customer satisfaction and loyalty.

Some ways firms might enhance the Decision stage include:

☆Streamlining the buying process: Making it simple for consumers to finish a purchase is crucial. This might involve giving clear and simple information about the product or service, as well as a secure and user-friendly checkout experience.

☆Offering numerous payment options: Allowing clients to pay using their chosen way, such as credit card, PayPal, or even through a monthly subscription, might boost the chance of a transaction.

☆Providing exceptional customer service: Having educated and friendly customer care personnel may make a major impact during the Decision stage. They can assist consumers with any queries or issues they may have and help them finalize their transactions.

☆Following up after the sale: Following up with clients after they make a purchase can help create customer loyalty and boost the chance of repeat business. This might involve sending a confirmation email, a follow-up call, or even a thank-you card.

By offering a pleasant client experience throughout the Decision stage, organizations boost customer happiness, establish customer loyalty, and increase the odds of recurring business.

In addition, organizations can also utilize data and analytics to analyze consumer behavior and preferences throughout the Decision stage, which can give useful insights for future sales and marketing efforts. This can help organizations discover any issues or hurdles that consumers have during the Decision stage and take efforts to enhance the customer experience moving ahead.

The Decision stage is a vital element of the customer journey and firms need to understand the aspects that impact a client's decision-making process.

☆Price: For many clients, price is a crucial component in their purchase choice. By offering clear and competitive price information, companies can make it easy for consumers to assess their alternatives and make a purchase.

☆Trust and reputation: Trust and reputation play a key part in the Decision stage since consumers are more inclined to acquire a firm they trust and that has a good reputation. Businesses can develop trust and reputation by offering exceptional customer service, delivering high-quality goods and services, and reacting to consumer feedback in a fast and efficient way.

☆Product features and advantages: Understanding the characteristics and benefits that are most important to consumers is vital to achieving a successful sale. By emphasizing the major advantages and characteristics of the product or service, companies can assist consumers to make an educated buying choice.

☆Urgency: Creating a feeling of urgency also impact the Decision stage, as clients may be more inclined to buy if they feel they need to move immediately. This might involve giving limited-time specials or discounts or stressing the restricted availability of a product or service.

☆Emotional connection: Finally, companies also develop an emotional connection with consumers by sharing tales and illustrating the influence that the product or service can have on their life. This help clients perceive the value of the product or service and make a purchase based on that relationship.

By considering these elements and understanding the client's viewpoint during the Decision stage, companies can enhance their chances of making a successful sale and creating customer connections.

Businesses need to understand the buyer's journey since it may help them design a more successful sales and marketing plan. By knowing the distinct phases of the trip, organizations can modify their message and strategy to fit the demands of each step.

For example, at the awareness stage, a firm can employ instructional content to educate prospective clients about its product and the issue it addresses. In the consideration stage, the firm could offer case studies or testimonials to emphasize the advantages of their product. And at the decision stage, the firm could provide special deals or incentives to urge the consumer to make a purchase.

By matching their sales and marketing activities with the buyer's journey, firms may establish a more successful and efficient sales process, and ultimately, generate more sales.

The buyer's journey is a critical idea for organizations to grasp because it can help them better understand their consumers and establish a more efficient sales and marketing plan. By knowing the many phases of the trip, organizations can modify their message and strategy to match the demands of each step and give the correct information at the right time.

It's also crucial to note that the buyer's journey might vary based on the sort of goods or services being offered and the particular consumer. For example, a consumer purchasing a high-end luxury automobile could go through a more complicated and in-depth buyer's journey than a person buying a simple home item.

To successfully interact with consumers at each point of the journey, organizations need to offer relevant and valuable content that solves their wants and queries. This may be blog articles, videos, infographics, case studies, or other sorts of material. The purpose is to educate, enlighten, and establish trust with the consumer so that they are more likely to pick the business's product or service over a competitor's.

In addition, firms can utilize multiple marketing channels and methods to contact clients at each point of the trip. For example, businesses utilize social media to reach consumers in the awareness stage, email marketing to connect with customers in the consideration stage, and retarget advertising to reach customers who have previously shown interest in the decision stage.

The buyer's journey is a dynamic and complicated process that needs organizations to understand their clients and design a unique strategy for each step. By doing so, firms can establish a more effective and efficient sales process, and achieve greater sales success.

Understanding Customer Needs and Pain Points

The understanding client wants and pain areas are crucial to offering relevant and successful sales solutions. It enables companies to:

- ***Identify opportunities***

Identifying opportunities requires examining the market and customer demands to discover places where there is a gap between what consumers need and what is already provided. By doing this, organizations can uncover new areas where they can deliver value and distinguish themselves from the competition.

For example, if a firm recognizes that consumers are asking for a quicker, more convenient delivery alternative, it might launch a new delivery service that satisfies this requirement. This may help the firm stand out from rivals and boost client happiness, eventually leading to greater sales and income.

To find opportunities, firms should frequently obtain and evaluate consumer data, and keep up-to-date on industry developments and client preferences. This information can assist organizations to determine where there are unmet requirements, and how they can build new goods or services to fulfill these needs and achieve a competitive edge.

- ***Improve product offers***

Improving product offers is an essential step in addressing client wants and keeping ahead of the competition. By receiving client feedback, companies can acquire vital insights into what consumers want and need from their goods and services. This can help organizations make educated choices regarding product design and development, and generate offers that are more attractive to consumers.

For example, if a firm gets input from clients that they want a product to be more portable, it may consider this feedback throughout the product design process and make adjustments to make the product more portable. This can assist the firm to satisfy consumer wants and boost customer happiness, leading to greater sales and income.

Improving product offers also help organizations remain ahead of the competition. By listening to consumer input and making modifications to goods and services to satisfy customer wants, firms can produce solutions that are more attractive and more differentiated than those of rivals. This may help organizations remain competitive and earn a greater portion of the market.

- *Tailor message and sales strategy*

Tailoring messages and sales methods to match the demands of various consumer groups is an effective strategy to increase the efficacy of sales and marketing operations. By segmenting clients based on common features and then personalizing messages and sales strategy to each segment, organizations can give a more relevant and customized experience to each customer.

For example, if a corporation has identified two consumer segments: one that values convenience and another that values quality, it might modify its message and sales technique to stress convenience for the first group and quality for the second. This can help the organization better satisfy the requirements and expectations of each group and boost customer satisfaction.

Tailored messages and sales methods also help organizations stand out from the competition. By offering a tailored experience to each consumer, companies distinguish themselves from rivals and establish stronger customer connections. This will lead to enhanced client loyalty, higher customer retention, and increased sales and income over time.

- ***Build trust and credibility***

Building trust and credibility with consumers is vital for success in the sales game. By displaying a thorough awareness of consumer wants and pain issues, firms should position themselves as experts in their sector and demonstrate that they have the client's best interests in mind. This can assist develop strong, long-lasting customer connections and make it more probable that consumers will pick the business's goods and services over those of their rivals.

For example, if a firm can show a deep grasp of a client's problem points and give a solution that successfully solves those pain points, the consumer is likely to see the organization as a trusted and reputable resource. This can lead to improved consumer loyalty and repeat business over time.

Additionally, by creating trust and credibility with clients, organizations may also boost the efficacy of their sales and marketing operations.

Customers are more willing to listen to and connect with firms that they trust, making it simpler to sell goods and services and expand the company over time.

- ***Increase client satisfaction***

Client satisfaction is a critical aspect of the sales game, as it encourages repeat business and helps to develop strong, long-lasting customer connections. By offering solutions that successfully address consumer wants and pain spots, organizations may not only boost customer happiness but also distinguish themselves from their competition.

For example, if a firm can identify a client's pain points and deliver a solution that successfully solves those pain points, the consumer is likely to be highly delighted with the experience. This may lead to improved client loyalty, repeat business, and favorable word-of-mouth referrals, which can help the firm develop over time.

Additionally, by concentrating on customer happiness, organizations also enhance the customer experience, which can lead to greater consumer engagement and better levels of customer loyalty. This, in turn, create more sales and income for the firm over time.

To understand client wants and pain areas, organizations might do market research, gather customer feedback, and analyze customer behavior and data. This information can be utilized to guide product development, marketing, and sales strategies, and enhance the customer experience.

☆Market research: Market research is a systematic method of acquiring, evaluating, and interpreting data relating to customers, market trends, competitors, and other variables. This information may be utilized to obtain insights into client wants and pain areas, as well as to uncover market possibilities and obstacles.

☆Customer feedback: Customer feedback is a useful source of information regarding customer demands and problem issues. Businesses gather consumer feedback via surveys, focus groups, customer service encounters, and other means. This input will be used to identify areas where consumers are unsatisfied, and to make modifications that better fulfill their requirements.

☆Customer data analysis: Customer data gives significant insights into customer behavior, preferences, and pain concerns. By evaluating customer data, organizations may obtain a better knowledge of consumer demands, and utilize this information to influence sales and marketing strategies, enhance the customer experience, and raise customer satisfaction.

☆Collaboration with other departments: Collaborating with other departments, such as product development, marketing, and customer support, also help organizations obtain a deeper knowledge of client wants and problem issues. By exchanging information and working together, these divisions help firms create more effective solutions that better fulfill client demands.

Understanding client wants and pain areas are key to offering relevant and successful sales solutions. By obtaining and analyzing information about consumers, organizations can acquire insights into what their customers need and desire, and use this knowledge to guide their sales strategy and enhance the customer experience.

Building Empathy and Connections with Customers

Building empathy and relationships with clients is a powerful means of understanding their requirements, pain areas, and motivations. Empathy is the capacity to comprehend and share the sentiments of others, and when utilized in a sales situation, it helps the salesperson to view things from the customer's perspective and better understand their requirements.

By creating empathy and relationships with consumers, salespeople can acquire insights into what inspires the customer, what their pain points are, and what they need to make a purchase. This information may then be utilized to alter the sales strategy and message to be more relevant and successful.

Additionally, creating empathy and relationships with consumers also assist to create trust and credibility, which can lead to better customer satisfaction and a higher possibility of closing a sale. It also helps to develop long-term client connections, which may lead to repeat business and strong word-of-mouth referrals.

Creating empathy and relationships with consumers is a key aspect of the sales game, as it helps salespeople better understand their clients and modify their approach appropriately, leading to higher outcomes and more customer happiness.

Chapter 2: Crafting Your Unique Sales Pitch

Crafting your distinctive sales pitch entails establishing a message that successfully conveys the value you give to your prospective consumers, and sets you apart from your competition. A good sales proposal should:

- *Identify the customer's needs:* Start by knowing your target audience and the difficulties they are seeking to address. This will help you personalize your pitch to their requirements and make it more relevant.

- *Highlight your unique value proposition:* Explain why your product or service is superior to others in the market and what sets it apart.

- *Emphasize the benefits:* Focus on the outcomes and results that your product will deliver to the consumer, rather than merely its features.

- *Be concise:* Your sales presentation should be brief, to the point, and simple to grasp. Avoid using technical jargon or sophisticated terminology that your readers may not be acquainted with.

- ***Use storytelling:*** People are naturally attracted to tales, and utilizing a fascinating narrative to explain your point may make your pitch more memorable and engaging.

- ***Practice:*** Rehearse your pitch until you are confident and comfortable presenting it.

Remember, your sales presentation should represent your personality and style, and be flexible to varied circumstances and audiences. The idea is to generate a message that connects with your prospective consumers and drives them to take action.

Defining Your Unique Selling Proposition (USP)

A Distinctive Selling Proposition (USP) is a statement that outlines what makes your product or service unique and different from your competition. It shows the advantages and value that your clients may anticipate from picking your solution above others in the market. A good USP may be a powerful tool for attracting your target audience's attention and establishing your brand as the best solution for their requirements.

Here are some stages for establishing your USP:

☆Identify your target audience: Knowing who your consumers are and what they are searching for is the first step in building a USP that connects with them.

☆Analyze your competition: Study your competitors' offerings and determine what they do well and what they don't. Use this information to identify what distinguishes your product or service distinct from theirs.

☆Define your value proposition: Determine what advantages your product or service gives to your clients and why they should select it over others.

☆Make it unique: Your USP should be a statement that cannot be repeated by your competition. It should be distinctive to your product or service and highlight its major features and value.

☆Test and refine: Test your USP with your target audience and obtain feedback. Use their ideas to enhance your USP and make it even more powerful.

A well-defined USP may be a crucial component in acquiring and maintaining clients. It should be clear, simple, and memorable, and be implemented into all elements of your marketing and sales operations.

- **_Understanding the Characteristics of a Strong USP_**

A good Unique Selling Proposition (USP) contains three essential elements that make it useful in distinguishing your product or service and grabbing the attention of your target audience:

☆Unique: Your USP should express what sets your product unique from your competition and why buyers should select it.

☆Relevant: Your USP should be immediately relevant to your target audience and solve their unique demands and pain areas.

☆Memorable: Your USP should be straightforward, memorable, and easy to recollect. A strong USP stays in the memory of your target audience and helps them remember your brand.

☆Precise: Your USP should be specific, underlining the unique advantages and value that your product or service delivers. Avoid generic or ambiguous remarks.

☆Verifiable: Your USP should be founded on facts and be verifiable by your consumers. Avoid making statements that cannot be substantiated.

☆Constant: Your USP should be consistent throughout all your marketing and sales activities, generating a strong and identifiable brand image.

☆Actionable: Your USP should motivate your target audience to take action, encouraging them to select your product or service above others.

Having a strong USP is vital for developing a successful brand and providing a competitive edge in your market. It should be a vital feature of your marketing plan, presented consistently across all your touchpoints with your target audience.

- ***Differentiating Yourself from Competitors***

Differentiating oneself from rivals is the act of building a distinct and compelling value proposition that sets your product or service apart in the market. Here are some strategies to help you separate yourself from your competitors:

☆Know your competition: Conduct comprehensive market research to discover who your competitors are and what they provide.

☆Identify your distinctive strengths: Determine what makes your product or service different, such as high quality, innovative features, great customer service, etc.

☆Know your target audience: Understand your target clients' wants and preferences, and personalize your solutions to fit their requirements.

☆Create a compelling value proposition: Use your unique capabilities and target audience data to build a clear and compelling value offer that separates you from your competition.

☆Leverage your brand: Develop a powerful and distinctive brand image that represents your unique value proposition and helps you stand out in the market.

☆Focus on the customer experience: Create a good and memorable customer experience that provides value and sets you apart from your competition.

☆Consistently innovate: Stay ahead of your competition by continuously inventing and upgrading your products to satisfy changing market requirements and client desires.

Differentiating yourself from your competition is a continual activity, involving a thorough awareness of your market and clients, and a dedication to offering excellent value.

Developing a Compelling Message

A captivating message is a clear and succinct statement of the advantages and value that your product or service gives to your target audience. It is a fundamental aspect of efficient marketing that helps you connect with your consumers, grow your brand, and accomplish your company objectives.

To further expound on producing an engaging message, here are some more considerations:

☆Use emotional appeals: A message that connects with clients' emotions is more likely to captivate their attention and leave a lasting impression. Consider employing comedy, empathy, or narrative to make your message more powerful.

☆Highlight distinctive aspects: If your product or service has unique features or capabilities, stress them in your messaging. This might assist to separate you from your competition and build a strong brand image.

☆Address consumer pain issues: Identifying and addressing client pain points is an excellent technique to generate a captivating message. By proving that you understand your consumers' concerns and giving a solution, you can create trust and credibility.

☆Make it actionable: A captivating message should motivate consumers to take action. Encourage people to test your product or service, make a purchase, or interact with your business in some manner.

☆Use client testimonials: Including customer testimonials in your messaging can be a great approach to developing trust and illustrating the advantages of your product or service. Testimonials gives social proof and indicate the value that your consumers have experienced.

☆Create a feeling of urgency: Using language that generates a sense of urgency can be an effective method to push clients to take action. For example, you may use wording like "limited time only" or "while supplies last" to create a feeling of scarcity.

☆Check and modify: Continuously monitor the efficacy of your message and alter it as required depending on consumer feedback and market developments. A captivating message should develop and alter over time to be current and successful.

By following these factors, you can build a message that successfully conveys the advantages and value of your product or service, separates you from your rivals, and resonates with your target audience.

- ***The Art of Storytelling***

The art of storytelling is the use of narrative to express information, ideas, or emotions. Storytelling has been used for millennia as a way of transmitting information and captivating people, and it remains a powerful strategy in contemporary marketing and communications.

Here are some components of good storytelling in marketing:

☆Identify a relevant protagonist: A protagonist that is relatable to your target audience can assist to develop an emotional connection and enhance engagement.

☆Establish a clear storyline: A good narrative helps to organize your tale and keep your audience interested. Consider adopting a clear, uncomplicated story that follows a beginning, middle, and finish.

☆Create an emotional connection: Feelings are a strong motivator, and a narrative that invokes emotions such as joy, grief, or excitement is more likely to be recalled.

☆Use colorful imagery: Vivid imagery can assist to bring your message to life and enhance engagement. Consider employing descriptive language and sensory detail to create a vivid and unforgettable experience.

☆Highlight key messages: Use your story to highlight the key messages you want to communicate to your audience, whether it is the benefits of your product or service or the values of your brand.

☆Make it memorable: A memorable story sticks with your audience long after they have heard it. Consider using memorable characters, surprising twists, or a memorable message to make your story memorable.

☆Use the power of brand storytelling: A well-crafted brand story can help to build trust, establish a unique brand identity, and connect with customers on a deeper level.

Incorporating storytelling into your marketing and communications efforts can help to engage your target audience, build trust, and achieve your business goals.

- ***Creating a Story that Resonates with Your Customer***

Creating a story that resonates with your customers requires a deep understanding of your target audience and their needs, wants, and pain points. Here are some tips for creating a story that resonates with your customers:

☆Know your audience: Take the time to understand your target audience by researching their demographics, interests, and behavior patterns. This information can help you tailor your story to their needs and interests.

☆Identify common challenges: Understanding the challenges that your target audience faces can help you create a story that resonates with them on an emotional level. For example, if your target audience is busy professionals, you might create a story that highlights the challenges of balancing work and personal life.

☆Show empathy: Empathy is the ability to understand and share the feelings of others. By showing empathy for your target audience, you can create a story that resonates with them and helps to build a deeper connection.

☆Use relatable characters: Characters that are relatable to your target audience can help to create an emotional connection and increase engagement. Consider using characters that embody the challenges and aspirations of your target audience.

☆Highlight the benefits: Your story should highlight the benefits of your product or service and demonstrate how it can solve your customers' challenges. Make sure your story is solution-focused and emphasizes the positive outcomes that your customers can expect.

☆Keep it simple: A straightforward story is more likely to resonate with your customers than a complex and convoluted one. Keep your story concise and easy to follow, and focus on a single message or theme.

☆Test and refine: Test your story with your target audience and refine it based on their feedback. This can help you ensure that your story resonates with your customers and achieves your desired outcomes.

- ***Using Storytelling to Illustrate Your Unique Benefits***

Using storytelling to illustrate your unique benefits is a powerful way to connect with your target audience and differentiate yourself from your competitors. Here are some tips for using storytelling to illustrate your unique benefits:

☆Identify your unique benefits: Take the time to identify the unique benefits that your product or service offers, and use this information to create a story that highlights these benefits.

☆Create a relatable protagonist: A relatable protagonist can help to create an emotional connection and increase engagement. Consider using a character that embodies the challenges and aspirations of your target audience.

☆Highlight the transformation: Your story should highlight the transformation that your product or service can bring about, and demonstrate how it can solve your customers' challenges. Use vivid imagery and descriptive language to bring this transformation to life.

☆Make it relevant: Make sure your story is relevant to your target audience and speaks to their specific needs and challenges. Consider tailoring your story to different segments of your target audience to ensure that it resonates with each group.

☆Keep it simple: A simple story is more likely to be remembered and have a lasting impact. Focus on a single message or theme, and keep your story concise and easy to follow.

☆Use emotional triggers: Emotional triggers are elements of your story that evoke emotions such as joy, sadness, or excitement. By incorporating emotional triggers into your story, you can increase engagement and create a memorable experience.

☆Integrate your brand: Integrating your brand into your story can help to build brand recognition and create a deeper connection with your target audience. Consider incorporating your brand values, mission, and personality into your story.

By using storytelling to illustrate your unique benefits, you can create an emotional connection with your target audience, differentiate yourself from your competitors, and achieve your marketing goals.

- ***Highlighting the Benefits of Your Solution***

Highlighting the benefits of your solution is an essential part of any sales pitch. Here are some tips for highlighting the benefits of your solution:

☆Focus on the customer: The benefits of your solution should be framed in terms of how they will benefit the customer, not just how they will benefit your business. Focus on the positive outcomes that your customer can expect and how your solution will solve their challenges.

☆Use specific, quantifiable benefits: Specific, quantifiable benefits are more compelling than vague or general claims. For example, instead of saying "our solution is faster than others," say "our solution can process transactions up to 50% faster than the competition."

☆Highlight the unique benefits: Highlight the unique benefits that your solution offers that are not available from your competitors. This can help to differentiate your solution and create a stronger value proposition.

☆Address common objections: Anticipate and address common objections that your customers may have, and explain how your solution will overcome these objections. For example, if your solution is more expensive than others, explain why the added cost is worth it in terms of the benefits it provides.

☆Use testimonials: Testimonials from satisfied customers can be a powerful tool for highlighting the benefits of your solution. Consider including testimonials from customers who have experienced the benefits of your solution first-hand.

☆Use visual aids: Visual aids such as graphs, charts, and images can help to bring your benefits to life and make them more memorable. Consider using visual aids to illustrate the specific benefits of your solution.

- ***Focusing on Customer Pain Points and Needs***

Focusing on client pain areas and demands is a critical component of crafting a good sales proposal. Here are some recommendations for concentrating on client pain areas and needs:

☆Understand your target audience: Take the time to research your target audience, their requirements, and the issues they confront. This information will be important in assisting you to discover their pain spots and build a solution that solves them.

☆Identify the pain points: Identify the primary pain points that your target audience encounters, and understand why these pain points are essential to them. Consider doing surveys, focus groups, or one-on-one interviews to acquire this information.

☆Position your solution as the solution: Once you have discovered your target audience's pain points, position your solution as the answer to these pain points. Show how your solution will address their difficulties and satisfy their demands.

☆Emphasize the advantages: Emphasize the benefits of your solution, and describe how it will enhance the lives of your target audience. Focus on the exact results that your target audience might anticipate, and utilize specific, quantitative advantages to make your argument.

☆Address the emotional aspect of the pain points: Pain points are not merely practical issues, they also frequently have an emotional component. Address this emotional component by expressing empathy for your target audience's predicament and explaining how your solution will not only address their practical issues but also enhance their emotional well-being.

☆Show the cost of inaction: Demonstrate the cost of not addressing the pain spots. Explain how neglecting the pain points will lead to poor effects for the consumer and underline the importance of finding a solution.

By concentrating on consumer pain spots and wants, you can develop a compelling case for your solution, distinguish yourself from your competition, and raise the odds of a successful sale.

- *Emphasizing Your Unique Differentiators*

To produce a sales presentation that genuinely connects with your consumers and sets your solution apart from your competition, it's crucial to concentrate on your distinct differentiators and to properly explain these differentiators to your customers. Here are a few other strategies to assist you to accentuate your distinct differentiators:

☆Make it personal: Personalize your sales presentation by adapting it to the unique demands and pain areas of your target audience. Use language that appeals directly to the consumer, and stress how your solution will address their unique difficulties.

☆Use visual aids: Visual aids such as infographics, movies, and product demos may help bring your distinct differentiators to life and make them more memorable for your consumers.

☆Answer objections: Anticipate and address any concerns that your clients may have regarding your solution and your distinct differentiators. Be prepared to present specific facts and explanations to back your arguments.

☆Be confident: Be confident in your solution and your distinct differentiators, and express this confidence to your customers. Let your consumers know that you believe in your solution and that you are enthusiastic about helping them overcome their difficulties.

☆Follow up: Follow up with your clients after your sales presentation to highlight your distinct differentiators and to address any further questions they may have. This follow-up will assist create trust and strengthen your connection with the consumer.

By following these recommendations, you can successfully explain your unique differentiators to your consumers and construct a sales presentation that sets your solution apart from your competition. Remember to constantly put your target customer and their requirements at the heart of your sales presentation, and customize your message to their unique difficulties and pain areas.

Presenting Your Pitch with Confidence

Presenting your pitch with confidence will substantially boost the efficacy of your sales presentation and help you win over your consumers. Here are some ideas for delivering your proposal with confidence:

☆Be prepared: Thoroughly prepare for your sales presentation by studying your target client, knowing their wants and pain areas, and anticipating any objections they may have. Rehearse your sales presentation multiple times to enhance your confidence and eliminate anxiousness.

☆Dress properly: Dress accordingly for your target audience and the sort of solution you are offering. Your look may have a big influence on the initial impression you create on your consumers.

☆Use body language: Use confident body language such as keeping eye contact, standing erect, and gesturing naturally and confidently. Avoid anxious actions such as fidgeting, crossing your arms, or avoiding eye contact.

☆Speak clearly and articulate: Speak clearly and articulate your words, and keep a constant speed and volume throughout your sales speech. This will help you deliver your message successfully and create rapport with your consumers.

☆Be enthusiastic: Be passionate about your solution and your distinct differentiators. Let your consumers know that you are sincerely involved in helping them overcome their difficulties and that you believe in the value of your solution.

☆Engage with your consumers: Engage with your customers by asking questions, listening to their comments, and adapting your pitch to their wants and problem spots. This will assist develop trust and enhance your connection with the consumer.

- ***Overcoming Nervousness and Anxiety***

It's normal to feel apprehensive or frightened before giving a sales presentation, but it's crucial to overcome these sentiments to properly express your message and develop trust with your consumers. Here are some strategies to assist you to overcome fear and anxiety while giving your sales pitch:

☆Practice: The more you practice your sales presentation, the more confident and comfortable you will become. Rehearse your sales presentation multiple times and receive feedback from trustworthy coworkers or acquaintances.

☆Concentrate on your audience: Instead of concentrating on your uncertainty or fear, focus on your audience and their requirements. This will let you connect with them and give them a solution to their difficulties.

☆Take deep breaths: Take deep breaths before you begin your sales presentation to calm your anxiety and steady your voice. Repeat this step if required throughout the presentation.

☆Visualize success: Visualize yourself giving your sales proposal with confidence and success. Imagine the good effects of your presentation and the delighted consumers who will benefit from your solution.

☆Remind yourself of your knowledge: Remind yourself of your expertise and the value that you deliver to your clients. Focus on the distinct differentiators of your solution and the advantages it brings.

- ***Preparing Mentally and Physically***

Preparing both emotionally and physically may considerably boost the efficiency of your sales presentation and help you deliver with confidence. Here are some recommendations to help you prepare emotionally and physically for your sales pitch:

☆Get a good night's sleep: A good night's sleep can help you feel rejuvenated and invigorated, enabling you to perform at your best.

☆Exercise regularly: Exercise can help you decrease stress and enhance your energy levels. Engage in physical exercise a few hours before your presentation to help you feel awake and focused.

☆Eat a good dinner: Eating a healthy meal before your presentation will help you maintain your energy levels and minimize symptoms of sluggishness.

☆Avoid coffee and sugar: Caffeine and sugar may enhance feelings of anxiousness and anxiety. Instead, go for water or herbal tea to help you keep hydrated and relaxed.

☆Meditate or perform yoga: Engage in mindfulness techniques such as meditation or yoga to help you calm your anxieties and remain focused.

☆Focus on positive self-talk: Use positive self-talk to improve your confidence and conquer emotions of uneasiness. Remind yourself of your knowledge and the value you provide to your clients.

- ***Building a Growth Mindset***

Building a growth mindset is a vital component of personal and professional development, and it can be especially effective in sales. A growth mindset is the notion that you can improve and progress through effort, experience, and learning. Here are some strategies to help you establish a growth mindset:

☆Embrace difficulties: View challenges as opportunities for development and learning, rather than as impediments.

☆Cultivate an optimistic attitude: Focus on the good parts of your sales proposal and your abilities, rather than obsessing about your faults.

☆Seek input: Seek feedback from colleagues, customers, and mentors to help you find areas for growth and build your talents.

☆Embrace failure: Embrace failure as a learning opportunity and a chance to develop and improve. Reframe setbacks as stepping stones to success.

☆Practice self-reflection: Regularly reflect on your performance and discover growth opportunities. Set objectives for your personal and professional growth and strive towards them.

By adopting a growth mentality, you will consistently develop your sales talents and create confidence in your abilities.

- *Using Nonverbal Communication and Body Language*

Nonverbal communication and body language can substantially affect the efficacy of your sales presentation and show your confidence, sincerity, and interest in your customer's demands. Here are some suggestions for leveraging nonverbal communication and body language successfully in your sales pitch:

☆Maintain eye contact: Make eye contact with your consumer to indicate attention, involvement, and sincerity.

☆Use open body language: Stand or sit with an open posture, with your arms uncrossed and your body facing the consumer. This might express confidence and approachability.

☆Avoid worried movements: Avoid nervous gestures such as fidgeting, tapping your foot, or fiddling with your hair. These might communicate fear or indifference.

☆Match your customer's body language: Try to match your customer's body language, such as their tone, speed, and posture, to develop a connection and build trust.

☆Use gestures and body language to highlight essential points: Use gestures and body language to emphasize key points and explain your message. For example, use hand gestures to show a product's characteristics or utilize facial expressions to indicate excitement or sincerity.

By employing nonverbal communication and body language successfully, you will boost the effectiveness of your sales presentation and develop a connection with your consumers.

- *Understanding the Power of Body Language*

Body language can be a significant tool in sales since it can indicate confidence, interest, sincerity, and more. Here are some of the primary ways that body language can affect your sales pitch:

☆Conveys confidence: Confident body language can express a feeling of authority, expertise, and trustworthiness, which can assist develop rapport with your consumer and boost the possibility of a sale.

☆Builds rapport: Matching your customer's body language, such as their tone, speed, and posture, may assist develop connections and build trust as mentioned before.

☆Communicates interest: Maintaining eye contact, nodding, and leaning in will indicate interest and participation in the discussion, making your consumer feel heard and appreciated.

☆Conveys authenticity: Employing open body language, avoiding anxious motions, and using gestures and body language to stress essential points will help express sincerity and genuineness.

☆Enhances the impact of your message: Using body language to underline important points and illustrate your message can make your sales speech more memorable and compelling.

By understanding the power of body language, you can utilize it to increase the effectiveness of your sales presentation and develop deeper connections with your consumers.

- ***Projecting Confidence via Posture and Gestures***

Posture and gestures can have a major influence on the impression of your confidence and trustworthiness during a sales presentation. Here are some suggestions for displaying confidence via posture and gestures:

☆Stand tall: Stand up straight with your shoulders back and head held high. This expresses confidence and authority.

☆Use confident movements: Use gestures that are confident and aggressive, such as utilizing an open hand to convey a point or using hand motions to demonstrate a product's qualities.

☆Avoid anxious movements: Avoid nervous gestures like fidgeting, tapping your foot, or messing with your hair, which might express worry or indifference as stated before.

☆Maintain eye contact: Maintain eye contact with your consumer to indicate attention and involvement.

☆Match your customer's posture: Try to match your customer's posture and gestures, such as their tone, pace, and posture, to develop a connection and build trust.

By displaying confidence via posture and gestures, you will boost the efficacy of your sales presentation and develop deeper connections with your consumers.

- *Engaging the Customer with Active Listening*

Active listening is a key aspect of good sales communication, as it helps create rapport and understanding with your consumer. Here are some suggestions for engaging the consumer via active listening:

☆Paying Attention to the Customer's Words and Tone

Paying attention to the customer's words and tone can provide you with significant insights into their requirements, goals, and motivations. Here are some recommendations for paying attention to the customer's remarks and tone:

◇Listen for keywords: Pay attention to terms that your consumer mentions, such as particular pain issues, objectives, or objections, which may provide you insight into their wants and motives.

◇Note tone of voice: The tone of voice can express the customer's feelings, such as joy, irritation, or skepticism. Paying attention to tone might help you comprehend the customer's viewpoint and react properly.

◇Watch for body language: Observing the customer's body language, such as posture, gestures, and facial expressions, can also provide you with indications about their mood and degree of interest.

By paying attention to the customer's words and tone, you will acquire a better knowledge of their position and reply in a manner that fits their requirements and answers their worries.

☆Reflecting on the Customer's Thoughts and Worries: By reflecting on the customer's thoughts and concerns, you can gain a better knowledge of their position, establish trust, and indicate that you're involved and devoted to finding a solution that fulfills their requirements. Remember to repeat back crucial points, paraphrase, answer objections, and demonstrate empathy to mirror the customer's ideas and worries in your sales profession.

☆Responding with Relevance and Empathy

Responding to your consumer with relevancy and empathy can help develop rapport and generate trust, leading to a stronger connection and better sales results. Here are some strategies for replying with relevancy and empathy:

◇Listen actively: Listen aggressively to the customer's requirements, problems, and objections to grasp their viewpoint and answer accordingly.

◇Address the customer's needs: Respond with relevance by addressing the customer's needs, desires, and worries, and delivering solutions that fulfill their requirements.

◇Show empathy: Show empathy by recognizing the customer's predicament, confirming their viewpoint, and understanding their feelings and motives.

◇Personalize the solution: Personalize your solution to the customer's individual needs, goals, and worries to show that you understand their position and that your solution is designed to match their criteria.

By reacting with relevance and empathy, you will develop a better connection with the consumer, establish trust, and boost the probability of a successful transaction

Chapter 3: Building Strong Relationships

Building great connections with customers is a vital aspect of success in sales. Here are some other advice and tactics for creating successful relationships:

☆Build rapport: Build rapport through identifying common ground, building a personal connection, and making the consumer feel appreciated and understood.

☆Personalize your approach: Personalize your approach to each client, taking into consideration their individual needs, desires, and worries, and giving solutions that are suited to their particular requirements.

☆Be responsive: Be sensitive to the customer's demands and concerns, and be ready to answer their inquiries and give help.

☆Add value: Add value to your encounters with the client by giving relevant and valuable information, offering insights and knowledge, and displaying a dedication to their success.

☆Show real interest: Show a genuine interest in the client and their needs, desires, and worries, and be prepared to commit time and resources to understand their position and create solutions that fit their criteria.

The Importance of Relationships in Sales

Relationships are crucial in sales since they influence the success of a salesperson and the firm they represent. Here are a few reasons why connections are vital in sales:

☆Trust: Building trust with a consumer is vital to developing a long-term partnership. Trust is developed through constantly delivering on commitments, being truthful, and providing solutions that suit the customer's demands.

☆Customer Loyalty: Strong connections can lead to customer loyalty, which leads to recurring business and favorable word-of-mouth recommendations.

☆Increased Sales: Customers are more likely to make a purchase when they sense a strong bond with the salesperson and the firm they represent.

☆Problem-Solving: Relationships allow for open and honest communication, which can help detect and address problems before they become big concerns.

☆Understanding: Building relationships allows salespeople to understand the customer's needs, desires, and worries, enabling them to give solutions that fit the customer's criteria.

Relationships play a critical part in sales as they help develop trust, boost client loyalty, drive sales, enable problem-solving, and give a better knowledge of the customer's demands. Investing time and effort in creating excellent connections with clients will pay off in the long run with improved revenue and a solid reputation for the firm.

Building Trust with Customers

Building trust with consumers is a vital component of sales since it establishes the basis for a long-term connection. Here are some recommendations and tactics for creating trust with customers:

☆Be truthful: Be straightforward and honest in your relationships with consumers, and avoid making false promises or withholding crucial facts.

☆Keep your word: Consistently deliver on pledges and follow through on commitments, since this indicates your dependability and fosters confidence.

☆Listen actively: Pay attention to the customer's demands and worries, and indicate that you understand their position. This demonstrates that you care and are involved in their achievement.

☆Give value: Offer solutions that fulfill the customer's demands and provide value beyond the product or service being sold.

☆Build rapport: Build rapport through identifying common ground, building a personal connection, and making the consumer feel appreciated and understood.

- ***Being Honest and Transparent***

Being honest and truthful is vital in generating trust with clients and establishing long-term connections. Here are some reasons why honesty and openness are vital in sales:

☆Builds Trust: Customers are more likely to trust a salesman who is honest and straightforward in their dealings, as opposed to someone who is ambiguous or conceals key facts.

☆Increases Credibility: Honesty and transparency boost a salesperson's credibility and reputation, making them more trustworthy in the eyes of the consumer.

☆Promotes Loyalty: Customers are more likely to stay loyal to a salesperson and the firm they represent when they believe that they are being treated fairly and honestly.

☆Avoids Misinterpretation: Honesty and openness help prevent miscommunication and misunderstandings, resulting in more productive and good relationships with consumers.

☆Demonstrates Appreciation: Being honest and upfront tells the consumer that you respect their time and intellect, and that you are committed to their success.

Being honest and upfront is a crucial component of generating trust and establishing great connections with clients. By continually exhibiting honesty and openness in your contacts, you will raise your reputation, develop trust, and ultimately drive sales success.

- ***Delivering on Promises***

When making promises to consumers, it is crucial to be explicit and detailed about what you are committed to fulfilling. Here are some ideas for successfully delivering on commitments in sales:

☆Be practical: Avoid making promises that you cannot fulfill, and make sure that your commitments are reasonable and doable.

☆Communicate clearly: Communicate the contents of your commitment to the consumer, including any caveats or limits, to ensure that there is mutual understanding.

☆Set expectations: Set explicit expectations with the client about timetables, delivery schedules, and any other pertinent data.

☆Stay organized: Stay organized and monitor your commitments to guarantee that you are on track to deliver on your promises.

☆Follow up: Follow up with the client to verify that they are pleased with the fulfillment of your promise and to resolve any questions or problems that may emerge.

☆Accept responsibility: If you are unable to deliver on a promise, take responsibility for the situation and attempt to address it in a manner that is fair to the consumer.

Delivering commitments is a vital component of generating trust and establishing great connections with clients. By being explicit, detailed, and realistic in your commitments, and by properly communicating, organizing, following up, and taking responsibility, you can successfully deliver on promises and develop strong, long-lasting relationships with consumers.

- ***Being Reliable and Consistent***

Being trustworthy and consistent is a crucial component of creating solid connections with consumers and maintaining a favorable reputation in sales. Here are some strategies for being trustworthy and consistent in sales:

☆Meet deadlines: Make sure that you meet deadlines and deliver on time, as promised. This convinces them that you are reliable and trustworthy.

☆Follow through: Follow through on pledges and promises to guarantee that consumers can depend on you to deliver what you say you will.

☆Be constant: Consistently supply high-quality goods or services, and maintain a consistent level of customer care and support.

☆Maintain standards: Maintain high standards for yourself and your work, and strive for excellence in everything that you do.

☆Be reliable: Be dependable and accessible to consumers, and answer swiftly to their wants and concerns.

☆Be professional: Maintain a professional attitude at all times, and always behave in a manner that is consistent with your beliefs and standards.

Being trustworthy and consistent is a critical component of creating solid connections with clients and maintaining a favorable reputation in sales. By regularly providing high-quality goods or services, following through on promises, and having a professional manner, you will create trust and confidence with clients and become a trusted partner in their success.

Developing Strong Communication Skills

Developing good communication skills is key to success in sales. Effective communication can help you create solid connections with consumers, overcome obstacles, and complete transactions more successfully. Here are some strategies for building good communication skills in sales:

☆Listen actively: Pay careful attention to what consumers are saying, and ask questions to explain their requirements and problems.

☆Use plain language: Speak clearly and succinctly, using basic language that is easy for clients to grasp.

☆Be confident: Speak with confidence, utilizing good body language and tone of voice to deliver your message successfully.

☆Adapt your communication style: Adapt your communication style to fit the customer's communication style, and utilize strategies such as empathy and active listening to develop rapport.

☆Be persuasive: Use persuasive language and narrative to successfully express the advantages of your product or service.

☆Meet objections: Anticipate probable objections, and prepare effective solutions that address the customer's worries.

☆Practice: Regularly practice your communication skills by role-playing exercises, attending sales training classes, or working with a mentor.

Developing good communication skills is key to success in sales. By carefully listening, speaking clearly and confidently, adjusting your communication style, and employing persuasive strategies, you can create great connections with consumers and complete sales more efficiently.

- ***Active Listening***

Active listening is a strategy used in communication where the listener pays careful attention to the speaker and participates with them in a meaningful manner. Active listening is a key talent in sales since it helps you to better grasp the customer's requirements and worries, create rapport, and generate trust. Here are some items to consider while practicing active listening:

☆Listen with your full body: Use nonverbal clues, such as eye contact and nodding, to demonstrate that you are engaged and interested in what the client is saying.

☆Be present: Be present in the moment and don't allow your thoughts to wander or worry about what you're going to say next.

☆Avoid assumptions: Don't make assumptions about what the consumer is saying or what they mean. Instead, ask questions to explain and comprehend their position.

☆Keep an open mind: Avoid being defensive or closed-minded, and instead approach each conversation with an open mind and a desire to understand the customer's requirements and problems.

☆Practice active listening regularly: Active listening requires practice, therefore make an effort to actively listen in all of your contacts, both personal and professional.

- *Asking the Right Questions*

Asking the correct questions is a vital element of good sales communication. By asking insightful and relevant questions, you will better grasp the customer's requirements and problem spots, and customize your sales approach appropriately. Here are some pointers for asking the appropriate questions:

☆Start with open-ended inquiries: Open-ended questions, such as "What are your major challenges?" or "Can you tell me more about your present situation?" enable the consumer to voice their opinions and concerns openly.

☆Identify their wants: Ask questions that assist you to understand what the consumer is searching for in a solution and what their requirements are. For example, "What are your priorities when it comes to finding a solution?"

☆Clarify their complaints: If the consumer raises any objections, ask clarifying questions to grasp their viewpoint and resolve their worries. For example, "Can you tell me more about why you're not interested in our solution at this time?"

☆Ask probing questions: After the consumer has given their opinions, utilize probing questions to acquire a better knowledge of their requirements and motives. For example, "What precisely made you consider our solution?"

☆Stay focused: Avoid asking extraneous questions or diverting from the issue at hand. Stay focused on the customer's requirements and keep the discussion on track.

By asking the correct questions, you can develop a connection with the client, obtain a better knowledge of their requirements and problems, and ultimately boost the odds of making a deal.

- *Providing Relevant and Valuable Information*

Providing relevant and meaningful information to your consumer is a key element of gaining trust and establishing a good connection with them.

Here are some ways to assist you to deliver relevant and meaningful information to your customer:

☆Focus on their needs: Before you start offering information, be sure that you understand the customer's requirements and problem spots. This will assist you to give information that is relevant and beneficial to them.

☆Use visuals: Visual aids like infographics, charts, and presentations appropriately help you explain complicated information in a straightforward and easy-to-understand method. Use graphics to highlight the advantages of your solution and show how it addresses the customer's unique challenges.

☆Use case studies: Share real-world examples of how your product has benefited other clients in comparable circumstances. This will provide the consumer with a greater knowledge of how your solution will work for them, and assist establish confidence in your solution.

☆Provide resources: Offer extra materials like whitepapers, webinars, and e-books that the buyer may utilize to learn more about your product. This will indicate that you are devoted to their education and achievement.

☆Use testimonials: Share customer testimonials to illustrate to the consumer the experiences of others who have utilized your service. This will assist develop confidence and credibility in your solution.

By concentrating on the client's requirements, and utilizing graphics, case studies, resources, and testimonials, you can give relevant and meaningful information that will help you create a solid connection with the consumer and boost the chances of completing a deal.

Creating a Positive Customer Experience

Creating a great customer experience is a critical aspect of the sales process and can have a big influence on customer satisfaction and loyalty. Here are some recommendations to help you establish a pleasant client experience:

- *Personalizing Your Approach*

Personalizing your approach is about building a relationship with your consumer on a deeper level, beyond merely selling a product or service. When you take the time to learn the customer's requirements, interests, and preferences, you can develop a connection of trust and credibility. This, in turn, improves the possibility that they will be interested in your solution and recognize the value in what you have to offer.

It's also crucial to remember that consumers nowadays are searching for more customized experiences, and they are more inclined to pick a firm that takes the time to understand their requirements and give solutions that are tailored precisely to them. Personalizing your approach can help you stand out from your competitors since many salespeople and firms still have a one-size-fits-all strategy.

Another advantage of personalizing your approach is that it can make your pitch and presentation more memorable. When you demonstrate that you understand the customer's problems and can give appropriate answers, they are more likely to remember you and your organization when they are ready to make a purchase.

Personalizing your approach is a vital component of developing great connections with consumers, generating trust, and separating yourself from your competitors. By taking the time to learn the customer's needs and adapting your message and presentation to their requirements, you will boost your chances of achieving a successful sale and developing a lasting connection.

- ***Being Adaptable and Responsive***

Being flexible and responsive involves being able to modify your strategy and message in real time depending on the customer's responses and comments. It's about being able to pivot and adapt to changes in the customer's demands, tastes, and interests, as well as being ready to reply swiftly to any questions, concerns, or objections they may have.

Having this flexibility and capacity to adjust is vital since no two sales circumstances are the same. Each consumer is unique and may have various wants, pain areas, and objections. Being flexible and responsive helps you to personalize your approach to each consumer, making it more likely that they will recognize the value in what you have to offer and be more open to your message.

Being adaptive and responsive also tells the consumer that you are listening and paying attention to their demands. This helps to develop trust and credibility since the consumer believes that you are involved in finding the best answer for them.

Being adaptive and sensitive is a fundamental component of being a good seller. By being adaptable and able to modify your approach depending on the customer's emotions and input, you will develop deeper connections, enhance the probability of completing a successful sale, and stand out from your competitors.

- ***Building a Long-Term Relationship***

In sales, creating a long-term connection with clients is crucial to preserving and expanding your company. By generating a great customer experience and offering value, you can nurture trust and create a loyal customer base.

To develop a long-term connection, it's crucial to tailor your approach and react to each customer's demands. This might mean identifying their pain areas and adapting your proposal to solve them, as well as being adaptive and attentive to their inquiries and concerns.

In addition, being dependable and consistent in your words and behavior may help develop trust and preserve the connection over time. And by delivering on your commitments and being honest and upfront, you may further create and enhance your relationship with the consumer.

Chapter 4: Closing Deals and Achieving Success

Closing transactions and attaining success in sales is the ultimate ambition for many salespeople. To achieve this, it's necessary to understand the customer's demands and provide a convincing presentation that emphasizes the advantages of your product. This might entail leveraging narrative and stressing your unique differentiators, as well as highlighting the customer's problem areas and illustrating how your solution meets them.

Confidence and great communication skills are also crucial to completing agreements. This might involve displaying confidence via body language, carefully listening to the consumer, and asking the proper questions.

Creating excellent connections with customers can lead to repeat business and increased prospects for future sales. By generating a great customer experience, being flexible and adaptive, and offering value, you will develop trust and foster a long-term connection with the consumer.

Understanding the Sales Process

The sales process is a systematic strategy for selling that is followed by sales professionals to gain new clients and conclude transactions. It often consists of multiple phases, including:

☆Prospecting: This is the process of locating possible clients who may require your product or service.

☆Qualifying: During this stage, you examine the prospective customer's demands, budget, and decision-making power to see whether they are a suitable fit for your solution.

☆Wants Analysis: During this stage, you explore further into the customer's unique needs and pain issues to identify how your solution may assist.

☆Presenting: This is when you showcase your solution to the consumer and emphasize its unique advantages and features.

☆Handling Objections: In this step, you address any objections or worries the consumer may have regarding your solution.

☆Closing: This is the stage where you ask the consumer to make a purchase choice.

☆Follow-Up: After the sale, it's crucial to follow up with the consumer to confirm their pleasure and handle any post-sale problems.

The sales process might vary based on the product or service being offered, the industry, and the target consumer. Salespeople need to understand and master the sales process to successfully assist clients through the decision-making process and complete more transactions.

- *Qualifying Leads*

Qualifying leads is the process of examining prospective consumers to see whether they are a suitable match for your product or service. It helps to prioritize the sales process by concentrating on prospects who are most likely to make a purchase. This comprises obtaining information about their requirements, budget, decision-making process, timetable, and other aspects that might affect the sale. By qualifying leads, sales teams may be more efficient in their efforts, spending more time on high-quality prospects and less time on unqualified leads. This phase is critical in optimizing resources and boosting the chance of completing a deal.

- *Building Rapport and Understanding Customer Needs*

Building rapport and understanding consumer demands are essential phases in the sales process. When you create a solid connection with a client, you have a better knowledge of their pain spots and demands, which helps you personalize your sales presentation to their scenario. By displaying your real interest in their well-being and success, you will create trust and position yourself as a valued counselor, rather than simply a salesman. This not only raises the chance of completing the deal but also establishes the groundwork for a long-term connection and prospects.

- ***Presenting Your Solution***

Presenting your solution is an important time in the sales process when you exhibit the advantages of your product or service to the consumer. It is crucial to personalize your presentation to the unique consumer and their requirements, rather than adopting a general pitch. Start by identifying the customer's pain areas and the precise ways your solution solves them. Be careful to highlight the specific differentiators that set your solution apart from rivals. Use stories and examples to show the advantages of your solution and make it relevant to the buyer. Emphasize the return on investment and how your solution will assist the client reach their objectives. Presenting your answer with confidence and conviction will raise the chance of a favorable result.

- ***Overcoming Objections***

Overcoming objections relate to addressing and overcoming any issues or objections that a prospective consumer may have about your product or service. This may be done by:

☆Identifying the fundamental cause of the objection: identify the underlying worry or need that is motivating the objection.

☆Address the complaint directly and honestly: recognize the customer's problem and deliver a meaningful and compelling solution.

☆Provide proof and examples: utilize statistics, case studies, testimonials, and other supporting resources to illustrate the value of your solution.

☆Offer alternatives: if a consumer has a particular problem, try presenting alternate solutions that meet their concern.

☆Keep the talk pleasant: adopt a positive, solution-focused attitude and avoid getting defensive or combative.

☆Ask for the sale: after overcoming obstacles, ask for the customer's commitment to proceed ahead.

By properly addressing objections, you can create trust and illustrate the value of your product, eventually helping you complete more transactions and achieve success in sales.

- ***Closing the Deal***

Closing the deal is the last step of the sales process when the salesperson and the buyer agree on the terms of the sale and make a commitment to the transaction. It is the moment when the consumer agrees to buy the goods or services. This stage needs good communication skills, active listening, and the ability to overcome any residual objections the consumer may have. The closing process should be done with confidence and professionalism, emphasizing the value and advantages of the solution being presented, and resolving any last concerns the client may have. The objective is to provide a great experience for the consumer, leaving them feeling happy with their choice to buy.

Effective Sales Techniques

Effective sales tactics relate to the methods and strategies that salespeople use to influence and convince prospective consumers to acquire a product or service. These approaches may include:

- *Using a Consultative Selling Approach*

Consultative selling is a customer-focused technique where the salesman takes the time to understand the customer's objectives, pain spots, and goals, and then delivers a solution that solves those needs. The idea is to create a long-term connection with the consumer, rather than merely generating a one-time transaction. This method entails asking questions, actively listening, and offering relevant and helpful information to the consumer. By knowing the client's requirements, the salesperson may adapt their solution to satisfy those demands and deliver actual value to the consumer. The emphasis is on fixing the customer's issue, rather than merely selling a product or service.

- ***Building Urgency and Scarcity***

Building urgency and scarcity are sales strategies that try to create a feeling of urgency or scarcity in the mind of the consumer, making them believe that they need to act soon or risk losing the opportunity. This may be done in several ways, including:

☆Limited-time offers: Create a feeling of urgency by giving a limited-time bargain, such as a discount or gift with purchase.

☆Scarcity marketing: Telling the buyer that your product or service is in great demand and that supply is restricted, creating a feeling of scarcity.

☆FOMO (Fear of Missing Out): Tapping into the customer's fear of missing out on a terrific opportunity or experience.

☆Urgent language: Use words and phrases such as "limited time only", "last opportunity", and "now or never", to generate a feeling of urgency.

By establishing urgency and scarcity, salespeople may inspire clients to take action, make a purchase and complete the transaction.

- ***Creating a Sense of Partnership***

The "partnership" selling method focuses on creating a connection with the client based on mutual trust, understanding, and objectives. The purpose is to work together with the consumer to solve their issue, rather than merely selling a product. This strategy stresses the client's requirements and goals and frames the salesman as a trusted adviser who is there to assist the customer in succeeding. By developing a feeling of collaboration, salespeople can create a deep connection with the client, which can lead to long-term, mutually beneficial partnerships, and increased sales success.

Measuring and Improving Your Results

Measuring and improving your outcomes is a vital element of the sales process since it helps you to evaluate what works and what doesn't, and make adjustments appropriately. This can be done by measuring critical indicators, such as the number of leads produced, conversion rates, and the average sale value. You may also utilize customer feedback, surveys, and other data to understand the customer experience and suggest areas for improvement. Regularly analyzing your performance and making improvements to your sales technique will help you achieve better outcomes, boost client happiness, and ultimately generate more sales.

- *Tracking Your Sales Performance*

Tracking your sales success entails measuring and assessing your outcomes over time. This will help you evaluate strengths and weaknesses, establish which tactics are performing best, and make required modifications to enhance your performance. Some popular metrics to measure are the number of leads produced, the conversion rate of leads to customers, average sale value, and customer lifetime value. By frequently assessing your performance, you will obtain useful insights into your sales process and take proactive initiatives to generate growth and boost success.

- *Identifying Areas for Improvement*

To find development opportunities, it's vital to measure and evaluate several elements of your sales performance. This might include measures like conversion rates, average transaction size, and customer satisfaction ratings. By periodically examining these data and comparing them to your objectives, you may find areas where you need to improve. For example, if your conversion rates are lower than intended, you may need to focus on your qualifying process or your presentation.

If client satisfaction is poor, you may need to strengthen your follow-up procedure or customer service. By regularly measuring and evaluating your performance, you can make data-driven choices to enhance your outcomes and achieve more success in sales.

- ***Continuously Refining Your Strategy***

Measuring and enhancing your sales outcomes is a vital stage in sales success. By measuring your sales performance, you may obtain a clear knowledge of your strengths and limitations and discover development opportunities. This will help you make data-driven choices about your sales strategy and techniques, and adapt your approach to better match the demands of your clients.

To monitor your sales success, you may use a range of technologies, including sales dashboards, spreadsheets, and customer relationship management (CRM) systems. These tools can help you measure KPIs like lead conversion rates, average transaction size, and closing rates.

Once you have a thorough grasp of your sales performance, you can then identify areas for development. For example, if you notice that you are losing a large proportion of sales during the presentation stage, you may want to work on increasing your presentation abilities or the quality of your product demonstrations. Similarly, if you discover that your close rate is poor, you may want to concentrate on improving your closing tactics and creating deeper connections with your consumers.

By consistently improving your sales approach, you will enhance your outcomes, complete more transactions, and achieve long-term sales success.

Chapter 5: Staying Ahead of the Competition

Staying ahead of the competition means studying the market and your rivals, and consistently upgrading your approach. This might entail studying your rivals' goods and services, as well as their strengths and flaws. It is crucial to understand what makes your solution distinctive and how you can separate it from the competitors. By remaining educated and proactive in making modifications to your approach, you can stay ahead of the competition and preserve a competitive edge. Additionally, frequently soliciting consumer input and implementing it into your strategy will help you remain ahead of the competition by ensuring you are fulfilling client wants and surpassing their expectations.

Understanding Your Competition

Understanding your competition entails investigating and assessing the strengths, weaknesses, opportunities, and threats (SWOT) of your rivals. This information can help you separate yourself from your competition, as well as suggest areas where you can enhance your offers to better fulfill client demands. By keeping an eye on your competition, you can remain up-to-date on industry trends, acquire insights into client wants, and build tactics to win business in a competitive climate. This information will also help you adapt to changes in the market, modify your pricing and sales methods, and capitalize on new possibilities.

- ***Conducting Competitor Research***

Conducting competitor research entails obtaining information about your competitors, including their goods, services, pricing, marketing methods, and target consumers. This information can help you comprehend the competitive environment, identify strengths and weaknesses, and build ways to distinguish your product or service. To perform competition research, you can acquire information from several sources, such as the company's website, news releases, industry publications, and customer reviews. Additionally, you can visit trade exhibits and events, join online forums and communities, and speak to consumers who have utilized your competition's goods or services. The purpose of competitor research is to get a detailed awareness of the competitive landscape and to uncover chances to distinguish your product or service in ways that are important to your target consumers.

- *Identifying Your Competitors' Strengths and Weaknesses*

Identifying your rivals' strengths and shortcomings is a key aspect of keeping ahead of the competition and enhancing your sales approach. This information might assist you to understand what makes your rival effective and where they might be lacking. It may also help you uncover possibilities to distinguish your offering and position your product or service in a manner that sets you apart from your competitors.

To determine your rivals' strengths and shortcomings, you may perform market research and acquire data via numerous sources such as customer reviews, industry publications, and competition analysis tools. Additionally, you can also go out to your present customers and ask for their opinion on your competition and their services.

By analyzing your rivals' strengths and weaknesses, you will build tactics to utilize your strengths and overcome your competitors' shortcomings. This might help you stay competitive in the industry and reach your sales objectives.

Adapting to a Changing Market

To be successful in sales, it is vital to be adaptive and receptive to changes in the market. This includes changes in client requirements, industry developments, and the competitive environment. By being updated about these developments, and altering your sales plan appropriately, you can continue to match client expectations and remain ahead of the competition. To achieve this, you will need to consistently modify your strategy and develop new and unique methods to give value to your clients. This might mean investing in new technology, generating new goods, or increasing customer service. By remaining ahead of the curve and being adaptable, you can continue to develop and flourish in a changing industry.

- ***Staying Up-to-Date on Industry Trends***

Staying up-to-date on industry trends is vital in sales because it helps sales professionals understand what is occurring in the market, what their clients and prospects are interested in, and what issues they are encountering. This intelligence may then be utilized to construct a more successful sales plan, adapt your approach to specific clients and prospects, and give important insights that can help establish better connections.

For example, by keeping up with trends in your business, you can be able to uncover new goods or services that may be of interest to your consumers, or changes in consumer behavior that could affect their purchasing choices. Additionally, remaining educated about new technology, marketing strategies, and regulatory changes will help you stay ahead of the competition and make your sales strategy more successful.

There are various methods to remain up-to-date on industry trends, including visiting trade exhibitions and conferences, reading industry magazines, subscribing to industry news and analysis, and following thought leaders and influencers in your sector on social media. The key is to make it a priority and to be consistent in your efforts.

- *Being Open to New Ideas and Approaches*

Being open to new ideas and techniques is vital in keeping ahead of the competition in sales. The market and client demands are always shifting, and it's crucial to keep ahead of the curve to be competitive. By being open to new ideas and methods, salespeople can acquire new strategies, keep up-to-date on the newest trends, and enhance their performance.

This involves being receptive to criticism, attending training sessions and seminars, and searching out new knowledge and resources to assist develop their abilities and techniques. By consistently upgrading their abilities and learning new methods, salespeople can move ahead of the competition and boost their performance in completing agreements.

- ***Anticipating Customer Needs***

Anticipating client demands entails knowing the existing and future desires, needs, and pain points of your target audience. It requires remaining updated about market developments and staying responsive to client behavior and feedback. By anticipating client wants, you can promote your solution as a proactive, valued resource that is well-suited to their evolving requirements.

This helps you move ahead of the competition and retain a competitive advantage in the market. Additionally, it helps establish closer connections with consumers, as they exhibit a thorough awareness of their requirements and a dedication to helping them reach their objectives.

Continuously Improving Your Skills and Knowledge

The continuous growth of your abilities and expertise is vital for sales success, as it helps you remain ahead of the competition and better serve your clients. This involves remaining up-to-date with industry trends, attending sales training and seminars, and always searching out fresh knowledge and tools that will help you enhance your performance. By putting time and effort into growing your talents, you can establish a stronger foundation for success, remain relevant in a quickly changing industry, and offer greater outcomes for your clients and your organization.

Additionally, this drive to personal growth may indicate your devotion to your customers and your work, which can assist establish trust and promote deeper connections.

- ***Investing in Professional Development***

Investing in professional development is a continual endeavor to enhance your abilities and knowledge in your sector. This might involve attending conferences, seminars, and training sessions, as well as reading relevant books, articles, and internet resources. This sort of investment will help you keep up-to-date on the latest industry trends and best practices, as well as enhance your problem-solving and critical thinking abilities. Furthermore, it can help you build new and useful talents, better your competitiveness in the industry, and raise your confidence in your abilities. Additionally, it can also represent to your company or customers that you are devoted to your job and take it seriously, which can lead to new prospects for development and progress.

- ***Staying Motivated and Committed to Your Goals***

Staying motivated and devoted to your objectives is key to attaining success in sales. This entails establishing clear and realistic objectives, creating a pleasant and supportive work atmosphere, being organized and focused and consistently searching out chances for growth and development. It might be good to have a support structure in place, such as a mentor or coach, and to routinely reflect on your development and celebrate your triumphs.

Additionally, remaining active with the business and surrounding yourself with like-minded folks will help you stay motivated and focused on your objectives. It is also crucial to be flexible and adaptive and not be disheartened by setbacks and disappointments, since they may frequently lead to excellent learning experiences and possibilities for progress.

- ***Seeking Feedback and Receiving Constructive Criticism***

Staying motivated and devoted to your objectives as a salesman may be tough, but asking for feedback and taking constructive criticism can help.

Seeking feedback and accepting constructive criticism is a key elements of sales success. It helps you to find areas of improvement and make required improvements to your sales strategy, tactics, and plans.

Regular feedback may be received via customer satisfaction surveys, sales reports, one-on-one meetings with managers, and team assessments. It's crucial to be open-minded and non-defensive while getting criticism and to utilize it as a chance for growth and development.

Additionally, constructive criticism can help you understand a problem from a new perspective and encourage you to make better judgments in the future. It's crucial to accept criticism honestly, taking the time to grasp the underlying problem and finding methods to solve it constructively.

Ultimately, by requesting feedback and accepting constructive criticism, you will consistently enhance your sales talents, remain motivated, and attain your sales objectives.

Final Tips

Setting the optimal pricing for your goods or service is a tricky state of things. You have to select a pricing that will represent your manufacturing expenses as well as the value your purchasers have on your goods.

Final Hints

Think about your manufacturing expenses. These costs lie in both the constant and changeable expenditures to produce or offer your product or service. Fixed expenses include rent, salary, and property taxes - any outlay that doesn't fluctuate a great lot of the time. Variable costs oscillate depending on the measure of products produced or services given. They include raw supplies, hourly pay, sales commissions, sites, and ads.

Analyze your market. How much are people willing to pay for your product? Conduct market research to test your pricing system. See what competitors are charging. You could price your goods more than the average if you give superior service and products than your competition.

Assess your product's originality. See how closely your product matches a competitor's product. Consumers will be unwilling to pay more rates for your goods if they may spend less for a competitor brand.

Ascertain your product's price elasticity. Your product's elasticity is established by whether price adjustments result in changes in demand. For instance, if modest adjustments in pricing results in big changes in demand; your product is looked at to be elastic. All the same, if there is little change in demand even with major price adjustments, your product is inelastic. The higher the price elasticity, the closer you ought to price your items to your competitors' products.

Set a price. Take all these components into account before arriving at a choice.

Wrapping Up

Ask trade or business organizations for details on common pricing practices or average profit margins in your sector.

Use your pricing scheme to build a product picture. If you price substantially lower than rivals, people may conclude that your product costs less because it is inferior.

Alter your price. You could adjust your price, based on your aims. For instance, you may offer a reduced initial price for a limited time to attract a big number of new consumers.

If in doubt, the pricing is on the high side. It's usually simpler to decrease prices than to increase them.

Beware of undercharging. Lowering your pricing considerably below that of competitors will establish an incorrect image of your goods. Small firms can't afford to undercharge since they frequently can't create enough units to qualify for volume discounts. Therefore, their take on each transaction is minimal.

Thanks For Reading

We appreciate you reading our book. We hope you liked it and learned something. We propose you employ the concepts and guidance supplied in the book to boost your life and reach your aims. We respect your thoughts, so if you would only take the time to give a review on the website where you purchased the book, it would be very appreciated. Your review aids other readers in recognizing our book and picking it up properly. Again, I want to thank you for coming this far.

www.ingramcontent.com/pod-product-compliance
Lightning Source LLC
Chambersburg PA
CBHW052348220526
45465CB00003BA/1006